Acclaim for Richard Brassey's previous book
Ghosts! The Ultimate Guide for Ghost Hunters

'Inside are tales about how to keep ghosts away, spooky sounds,
famous hauntings ... all illustrated in the cheery style that made Richard
Brassey's *Brilliant Brits* such a hit among primary school historians'
– Amanda Craig, *The Times*

'Wonderfully well-designed and well-presented (in Brassey's)
inimical style, a title that will have wide appeal' – ACHUKA

'Easy to read and generously illustrated'
– Rosalind Kerven, *The Northern Echo*

'creepy ... but mitigated by the author's gently comic illustrations with
their amiable expressions ... There is enough spookiness here to stir
children's imaginations, but none of the images will haunt them'
– Nicolette Jones, *The Sunday Times*

FASTER
FURTHER

TRIUMPHS IN TRANSPORT

HIGHER
DEEPER

Other books by Richard Brassey

Ghosts! The Ultimate Guide for Ghost Hunters

The Story of London

The Story of Scotland

Nessie the Loch Ness Monster

Greyfriars Bobby

published by Orion Children's Books

FASTER FURTHER HIGHER DEEPER

TRIUMPHS IN TRANSPORT

RICHARD BRASSEY

Orion
Children's Books

a c

Copyright © Richard Brassey 2008

Designed by Louise Millar

The Orion Publishing Group's policy is to use papers that are natural, renewable
and recyclable products and made from wood grown in sustainable forests.
The logging and manufacturing processes are expected to conform to
the environmental regulations of the country of origin.

A catalogue record for this book is available from the British Library
Printed in Spain by Cayfosa - Quebecor

ISBN 978 1 84255 700 6

www.orionbooks.co.uk

CONTENTS

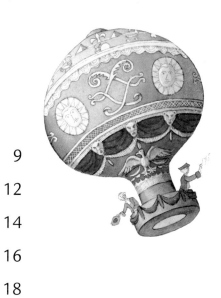

FROM **A** TO **B**:
faster, further, higher, deeper

Ever since they started to wriggle, living creatures have tried to outdo each other by going faster, further, higher, deeper.

Nobody knows exactly why our apelike ancestors first stood on two legs. For millions of years they ran as fast as they could after animals.

In fact it's thought that ancient peoples chased and ate all the horses in America without ever realising they could have been riding them.

But in Asia there were still plenty of horses and about 6,000 years ago somebody thought to ride one . . .

And about the same time somebody invented the wheel . . .

. . . and put it on a chariot, tied a horse to the chariot and went fast.

FASTER!

About 5,000 years ago the ancient Egyptians went faster by rigging sails on their ships. On the Nile the wind always blows south and the current flows north. They found they could sail north and use oars to row south.

FURTHER!

People had always migrated – in search of fertile land and for animals to hunt. As they settled and civilizations grew, they began to explore further and further from home in search of wealth.

In the early 1400s the Emperor of China sent thousands of huge junks to explore as far as they could go. Some of them may have gone right round the world long before anybody else.

In 1492 Christopher Columbus sailed across the Atlantic to discover the Americas for the King of Spain.

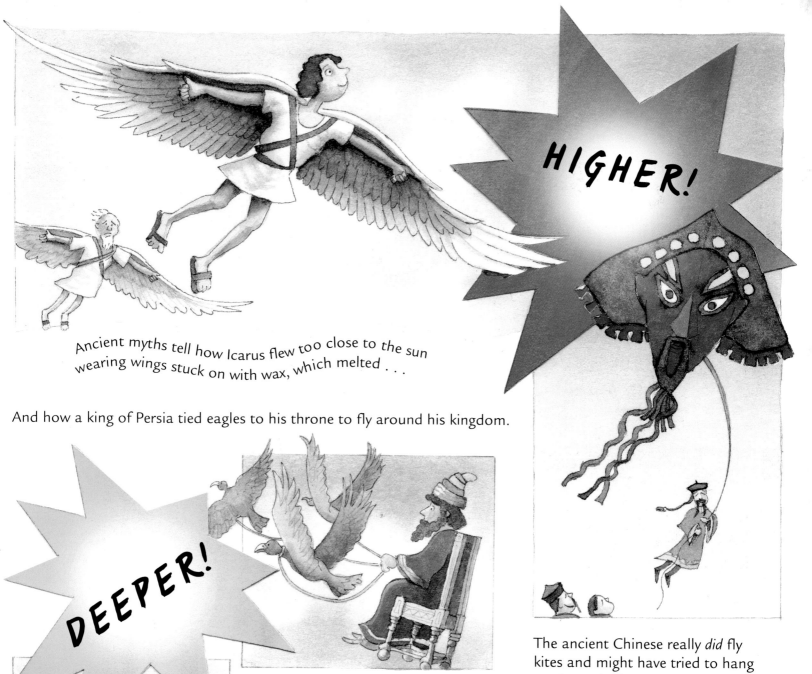

HIGHER!

Ancient myths tell how Icarus flew too close to the sun wearing wings stuck on with wax, which melted . . .

And how a king of Persia tied eagles to his throne to fly around his kingdom.

DEEPER!

The ancient Chinese really *did* fly kites and might have tried to hang on the end of one.

For thousands of years divers risked their lives to find rare and precious pearls at the bottom of the sea.

The earliest known submarine was a submerged rowing boat, which went up and down the Thames in 1623.

11

ALL STEAMED UP

When we travel anywhere today, it's almost always in a vehicle with an engine. It took nearly 2,000 years from the invention of the first engines until anyone managed to make an engine-powered vehicle.

JAMES WATT and the TEA KETTLE

British schoolchildren used to be taught this story:

In 1748 12-year-old James Watt was sitting in the kitchen watching the steam from a boiling kettle make its lid bounce up and down. When he pushed the lid shut, the steam came bursting out of the spout. On seeing this, he wasted no time in inventing the steam engine.

This last part of this story is nonsense. James Watt *did not* invent the steam engine, although he *did* improve it. But it does show the force of steam power to move things as it did the kettle lid.

> That's amazing!

The first we hear of steam power was 2,000 years ago when Archytas, a Greek, made a hollow pigeon from clay, filled it with water and heated it until steam shot out through a hole in its behind. This made it seem to fly along a wire.

The Greeks may also have made steam-powered moving statues to frighten enemies in battle.

A few hundred years later Hero, another Greek, built an aeolipile.

> That's amazing!

CREAK

This pointless contraption had nozzles attached to a disk. It shot out steam and made the disk spin. Some say Hero built a big version to open heavy temple doors.

One of the first people to try to make steam-powered vehicles was Sir Isaac Newton. In 1700 he fixed a steam jet onto a cart but the jet wasn't powerful enough and he went nowhere. At about the same time we first hear of steam being used to drive a wheel with a cylinder engine.

The first steam engines, which turned wheels, were used to pump water from mineshafts.

The PISTON and CYLINDER ENGINE

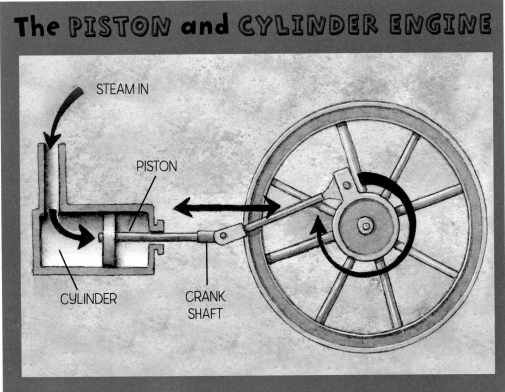

STEAM IN

PISTON

CYLINDER

CRANK SHAFT

A jet of steam is forced into a cylinder. Inside is a piston, which is pushed up and down just like Watt's kettle lid. The piston has a rod attached, which turns the wheel by a hinged crank-shaft.

BOOM!

It took a lot of fine-tuning – and explosions! – before safety valves were perfected so the pressure in steam engines could be controlled.

FASTER AND FURTHER WITH AN ENGINE!

Who was the first person to make a vehicle with an engine which worked ... and when? History is a bit confused.

1670 — THE FIRST CAR EVER?

Stories tell of Father Verbiest, a Belgian missionary, who astonished the Emperor of China by building a little steam-powered trolley car. If we could be sure this story was true, it would be the first ever self-propelled car ... but we can't.

1704 — THE FIRST EVER BOAT WITH AN ENGINE

In 1704, Denis Papin, a French doctor, put a piston and cylinder engine in a boat to drive some paddles – the first ever definite working vehicle with an engine. Unfortunately, some boatmen were so horrified by this newfangled, smoking monster that they destroyed it. Denis couldn't afford to build a new one. He gave up the idea and died penniless.

THE BONE DIGESTER and the STEAM VALVE

Fat and ground bones are very useful.

The force of steam can move things!

Sssssss!!

When Denis Papin put butcher's bones in a big sealed pot with water and heated it over a fire, the steam inside was so hot it melted all the fat off the bones. Denis had invented the pressure cooker. Trouble was, every so often his pots exploded. So he drilled a hole in the top and put a weight over it. If the pressure got too high, the steam was forced through the hole and lifted the weight to escape. Denis had a 'James Watt' moment. He went on to invent the piston and cylinder engine.

1770 — THE MONSTER STEAM CART CRASH

Nicolas Cugnot built machines for the French army but his hobby was making steam engines. In 1770 he built a huge engine with a drive wheel, which he put at the front of a cart (instead of horses) for transporting cannons.

Although the cart had to stop every ten minutes to get up steam, he reached the astonishing speed of two mph. That's slower than a man walks but it was too fast for Nic.

He lost control and lumbered through a garden wall. Even if Father Verbiest did beat him to making the first car, Nic definitely had the first car crash.

As with the first car, we're not sure who was the first person to fly. In Portugal they'll tell you it was Bartolemau de Gusmao who went up in a bird-shaped balloon in 1709, although the story goes, his balloon caught fire and came down in flames.

A LOT OF HOT AIR

Was it Montgolfier gas that lifted a sheep, a duck, a rooster and two men high into the air?

The Montgolfier brothers came from a family of sixteen. Joseph (no. 12) was untidy and shy but brilliant at inventing things. Etienne (no.15) was natty and smart and good at business.

I'll call it Montgolfier Gas.

One day Joseph noticed how some sheets billowed upwards while drying over a fire. He decided smoke must have something in it that lifted things. (We now know that hot air rises.)

Definitely Montgolfier Gas!

After several experiments the two brothers built a large box frame covered with silk on all sides except the bottom. Then they lit a fire underneath and watched it soar skywards. It fell to earth two kilometres away, where a passerby was so startled that he set upon it with his stick, ripping it to shreds.

Do let's try. They might explode!

Or melt so close to the sun!

Undeterred, they built an even bigger, round-shaped balloon. Etienne took it to Paris to show the King and Queen of France. In those days people imagined something terrible might happen to a person who flew too high. The King offered Etienne two criminals as an experiment to find out what!

Etienne decided he'd rather send up a duck, a cockerel and a sheep named Skyclimber. The balloon reached 300 metres. When it landed two miles away Skyclimber was still munching hay contentedly. The cock and duck, although seeming a little upset, were unharmed.

So two months later, in November 1783, the brothers sent up an even bigger balloon. On board were two volunteers - a doctor and an army officer. They landed safely nine kilometres outside the walls of Paris and could have gone further but the doctor put the fire out with his coat because he was worried it might set the balloon ablaze. This is the first time we can be certain that people really did fly.

THE BALLOON EXPLOSION

**Anything filled with hydrogen gas will float upwards.
Unfortunately it also bursts into flames at the slightest spark.**

Soon after the Montgolfiers' first manned flight in 1783, another Frenchman, Jacques Charles, filled a balloon with hydrogen and took off one rainy day in Paris. When he came back down through the dark clouds 24 kilometres away, some villagers thought his balloon was a sky monster and destroyed it.

Next year Jean-Pierre Blanchard and an American friend were the first people to fly the English Channel. At one point their balloon dipped so low they threw everything out of the basket.

They arrived in France wearing only their underpants.

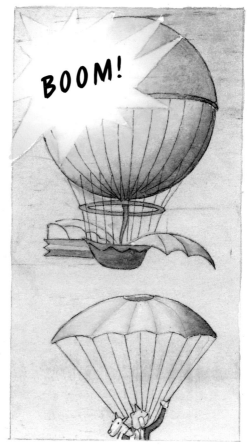

BOOM!

On another occasion his balloon exploded. The parachute saved Jean-Pierre's life.

Jean-Pierre tried flapping wings to control the flight of his balloon. He also invented the parachute, which he tried out first on his pet dog.

But the day J-P had a heart attack and fell over the side, he was not wearing his parachute. He toppled like a stone from the basket and was killed.

In 1819 Jean-Pierre's wife, Sophie, met a more spectacular fate when she took off with a basket full of rockets as part of a firework display above Paris. Instead of going sideways, the fireworks shot upwards, setting the balloon ablaze. It rose high in the air before plunging to the street below, where Sophie was dashed to pieces.

In 1852 another Frenchman, Henri Giffard, fixed a propeller driven by a steam engine below a cigar-shaped balloon. He only chugged along at five miles per hour ... but he *had* invented the airship.

Things *really* took off when the German Count von Zeppelin fitted an internal combustion engine to a rigid framed balloon and gave his name to this type of airship.

By the 1930s, Zeppelins were all the rage. Nearly as big as the ocean liner *Titanic*, the Hindenberg had cabins for 50 passengers, who were pampered by a crew of 40. For over a year it busily flew between Europe, the USA and Brazil.

THE HINDENBERG DISASTER

But then, disaster ... In May 1937, while trying to land near New York, the Hindenberg caught fire and the hydrogen exploded. Thirty-five people were killed. The rest managed to jump clear as it crashed to the ground in flames. The Hindenberg was the first such disaster to be captured on film. Her fiery end was seen all round the world. People were so horrified that it put an end to travel by airship. In any case, by this time aeroplanes were starting to take over.

THE RAILWAY BOOM!!

The age of modern transport really began when people thought of using steam engines to pull trains much further and faster on railway lines.

Around 600 BC King Periander built a railway to carry boats from one side of Greece to the other across the Isthmus of Corinth. It was made of stone blocks with grooves cut into them. He used slaves to pull the wagons.

The Romans built similar railways but used horses to do the pulling.

Richard grew up in Cornwall where there were lots of tin and copper mines, using both steam pumps and horse drawn railways. In 1801 he put a steam engine in a cart, called it the Puffing Devil and drove down the road with some friends.

They parked outside a pub for a lunch of roast goose, leaving the Puffing Devil's fire still burning. Suddenly, it blew up!

In 1803 Richard had the better idea of putting a steam engine on a wagon on a railway, normally worked by horses. This was the first ever rail locomotive. Unfortunately the iron rails kept cracking under the steam engine's weight so the mine owner went back to using horses. But it wasn't long before others began building railways with stronger rails.

THE RAINHILL TRIALS

In 1829 a railway was built from Liverpool to Manchester and a competition held to decide on the best locomotive to pull the carriages. There were five entries:

THE NOVELTY ...

reached 30mph in trials and was the favourite but a pipe burst so it withdrew.

SANS PAREIL ...

was rather old fashioned and used a lot of coal. Its pump broke so it withdrew.

PERSEVERENCE ...

broke down before even getting to the trials. When it did arrive, it only managed six miles per hour.

THE CYCLOPED ...

was two horsepower ... literally! It had no engine, only two horses in the wagon, walking on a treadmill.

STEPHENSON'S ROCKET ...

had many new features, which would be used in most locomotives from then on. It was the only engine to complete the 50-mile round trip, reaching 29 miles per hour.

BOOM!

A year later, at the railway's opening ceremony, William Huskisson MP was crossing the track and didn't realise how fast the Rocket was moving. He was crushed to death – the first man to die in a railway accident. Curiously, he'd already nearly been crushed to death once ... during his honeymoon years before when a horse fell on him.

The first locomotive to be built in the USA was the Best Friend of Charleston in 1830. Apparently, the fireman got so fed up listening to the whistle of the safety valve that he covered it with a large piece of wood and sat on it ... BOOM! The engine exploded into a thousand pieces hurling the fireman to his death.

BRUNEL'S GREAT BIG SHIPS

At 18, Isambard Kingdom Brunel was already helping his engineer father dig the first tunnel under the Thames. He went on to build railway lines, the most amazing bridges, and ships.

Sailing ships took a month to cross the Atlantic. Steamships were faster but nobody thought one could be built able to carry enough coal for the journey ... except Isambard. In 1838, *Great Western* set off to race across the Atlantic against a small channel steamer, named *Sirius*.

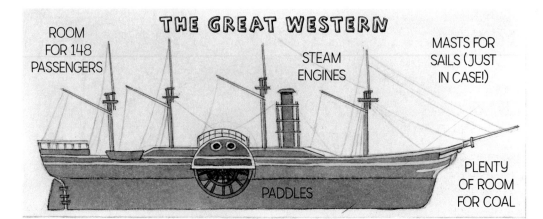

THE GREAT WESTERN

ROOM FOR 148 PASSENGERS

STEAM ENGINES

MASTS FOR SAILS (JUST IN CASE!)

PADDLES

PLENTY OF ROOM FOR COAL

Great Western had hardly left the Thames when smoke was seen pouring from the boiler room. Isambard rushed to fight the fire but the ladder had burnt away. He fell into the hold and was knocked unconscious.

The fire was put out and Isambard hauled to safety. But he had to stay behind when *Great Western* set off again. With such a start *Sirius* won, taking 19 days, although she ran out of coal and had to burn cabin furniture.

Great Western took only 15 days and had 200 tons of coal left. The crowds cheered as she entered New York harbour ... the biggest, fastest ship ever.

THE GREAT BRITAIN

SCREW PROPELLER

IRON HULL

Immediately Isambard made plans for a new ship. In 1845 *Great Britain* (twice the size of *Great Western*) crossed the Atlantic in 14 days. Unfortunately, she then ran onto some rocks off Ireland. Her compass was confused by all the iron in her hull.

THE GREAT EASTERN

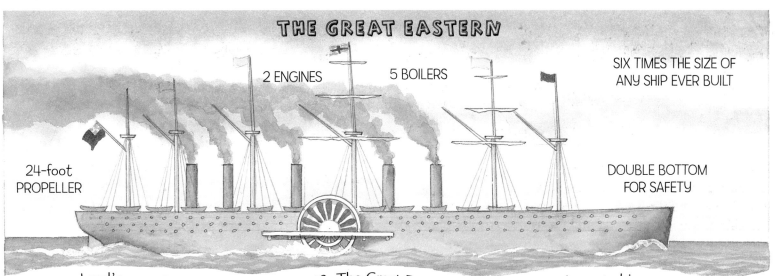

24-foot PROPELLER

2 ENGINES

5 BOILERS

SIX TIMES THE SIZE OF ANY SHIP EVER BUILT

DOUBLE BOTTOM FOR SAFETY

Isambard's next ship was launched in 1852. The *Great Eastern* became by far the largest ship ever built.

Such huge crowds arrived to watch that shouted instructions couldn't be heard. The ship slipped and a man was killed when a winch spun out of control.

Special steam rams had to be built and it took three months finally to launch her in the water.

BOOM!

Isambard had a stroke and was in bed at home when *Great Eastern* finally steamed down the Channel. Suddenly the first of the five funnels shot into the air like a rocket. Six stokers were scalded to death. But the great ship was so well built she kept going with only two boilers working. It turned out some workmen had left some valves closed, which should have stopped just such an explosion.

A few days later Isambard died. *Great Eastern* was kept very busy for the next 30 years, even laying the first telephone cable across the Atlantic.

THE DISASTROUS *TITANIC*

Everybody thought the ultra modern *Titanic* was unsinkable. But on her maiden voyage in 1912 she hit an iceberg and sank. One and a half thousand people were drowned. It's still among the worst passenger ship disasters ever.

Over dinner in London in 1907 the Chairman of the White Star Line and a Belfast shipbuilder decided they would build the two biggest and most luxurious ocean liners ever seen.

Huge and luxurious! ... and unsinkable!

White Star had a history of disasters. The worst was the *Atlantic* which sank off Nova Scotia in 1873, drowning 200 children. In fact, at that time, it was the worst passenger ship disaster ever.

First to be launched was *Olympic* which had a series of accidents. She squashed a tug in New York harbour, crashed into a Royal Navy cruiser and lost a propeller after hitting something in the Atlantic.

Captain Smith, who was in charge of *Titanic*, was well known for being reckless. The White Star Line wanted *Titanic* to go flat out on her maiden voyage to see what her top speed was despite warnings of icebergs.

It was night when she struck ice. At first nobody believed she could be sinking. There'd never been a practice drill and there weren't nearly enough lifeboats. In the chaos many were launched half empty.

There's all sorts of ideas about why the 'unsinkable' *Titanic* sunk. The ship broke in half as she went down.

It's thought the steel she was made from had become brittle at freezing temperatures.

Afterwards, safety in transport became something everybody talked about. Today travel is much safer because of all we learned from disasters like the sinking of *Titanic*.

EGGS AND ALLIGATORS

In the fourth century BC, Greek philosopher Aristotle wrote about a diving bell forced straight down into the water like an upside-down bucket.

In 1620 King James I is said to have gone for a ride under the Thames in a rowboat with a leather cover.

In 1690 famous scientist Edmund Halley spent an hour underwater with some friends in a diving bell supplied with air in barrels.

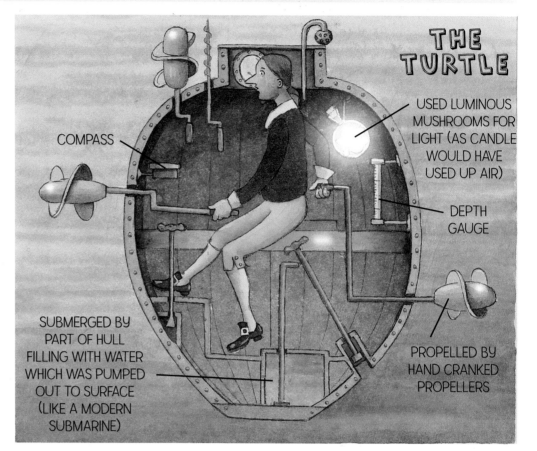

THE TURTLE

COMPASS

USED LUMINOUS MUSHROOMS FOR LIGHT (AS CANDLE WOULD HAVE USED UP AIR)

DEPTH GAUGE

SUBMERGED BY PART OF HULL FILLING WITH WATER WHICH WAS PUMPED OUT TO SURFACE (LIKE A MODERN SUBMARINE)

PROPELLED BY HAND CRANKED PROPELLERS

The *Turtle* was made by David Bushnell of Connecticut during the American Revolutionary War to drill holes in the bottoms of British ships so he could pop in a keg of powder and blow them up. Instead, he got lost underwater. He used a timer to explode the gunpowder anyway which caused the enemy to scatter in fright.

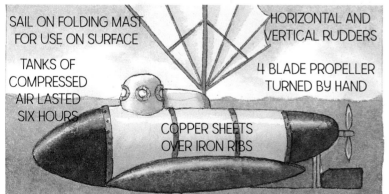

SAIL ON FOLDING MAST FOR USE ON SURFACE

TANKS OF COMPRESSED AIR LASTED SIX HOURS

HORIZONTAL AND VERTICAL RUDDERS

4 BLADE PROPELLER TURNED BY HAND

COPPER SHEETS OVER IRON RIBS

Nautilus was built in France in 1800 by American, Robert Fulton. It was much more like a modern submarine. After sinking a couple of ships in trials Napoleon decided he didn't want it. Bob offered it to the British, but they didn't want it either.

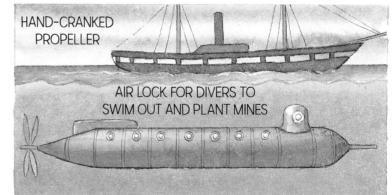

HAND-CRANKED PROPELLER

AIR LOCK FOR DIVERS TO SWIM OUT AND PLANT MINES

The *Alligator* was intended for use by the North in the American Civil War. It used compressed air and air filters so the crew of 20 could breathe. Unfortunately it sank in a storm while being towed, and never saw action.

PEDAL POWER

The first bicycles were made to measure according to how long your legs were ...

THE DANDY HORSE

Baron von Dreis invented his Dandy Horse in Germany in 1816. It was made of wood and had no pedals. The rider pushed against the ground with his feet. On the flat or going downhill, you got going fast enough and then lifted your feet and freewheeled. It became quite a craze, especially where there were smooth pavements in towns. This resulted in many collisions with pedestrians and a lot of towns banned them.

KIRKPATRICK MACMILLAN (1812-1878)

Kirkpatrick Macmillan was a blacksmith near Dumfries in Scotland. One day he was at work in his father's forge, when somebody rode by on a Dandy Horse.

Kirkpatrick immediately built himself one. Then, by attaching two pedals which swung back and forth to the rear wheel, he was able to pedal instead of scoot. In 1842 he rode 68 miles to Glasgow. It took him two days. At one point he even raced the stagecoach.

In Glasgow, he crashed into a small girl. Although she wasn't badly hurt, the magistrate fined him five shillings and then asked for a go on Kirk's bike.

Like many blacksmiths in those days, Kirkpatrick was also the village dentist ... for horses as well as humans! We can't be sure he was the first person to invent the bicycle. He certainly never took any credit or made money from it. Others soon copied and improved it and claimed it as their own invention.

THE PENNY FARTHING

Early bikes were known as boneshakers. Their metal tyres gave a very bumpy ride. They were also very hard work to pedal. James Starley, a Coventry sewing-machine maker, realized they could go much faster and be more comfortable with a front wheel as high as the rider's leg length and pedals on the hub. The only way to get on was to build up speed while running alongside, then jump. If you had to stop suddenly you got thrown over the handlebars.

BIKER BEGINNINGS

Motor bikes were the first vehicles to be fitted with a new type of engine which would change the world, but the first ones were steam-powered.

SYLVESTER'S STEAM MOTOR BIKE

In 1869, Sylvester Roper of Massachusetts made a wooden steam-powered motorbike. It had one cylinder on either side and a charcoal fire with a chimney behind the saddle. He annoyed the neighbours and spooked horses riding round town on this noisy and smelly machine.

When he was 73, Sylvester took his bike to Boston to race some students on pedal cycles. They scoffed at his smoky machine but, as soon as the race started, they were left far behind. Sylvester went even faster. At 40 miles per hour he went into a wobble, was thrown from the bike and died of a heart attack.

PETROL POWER

The first motor bike with a petrol engine was built in Germany in 1885 by Gottlieb Daimler and Wilhelm Maybach. It was also the first vehicle of any kind to be fitted with a modern internal combustion engine, which you can read about on the next page.

INTERNAL COMBUSTION ENGINE

Nobody could make a really good motor car or an aeroplane until an efficient internal combustion engine had been developed.

OTTO CYCLE FOUR-STROKE ENGINE

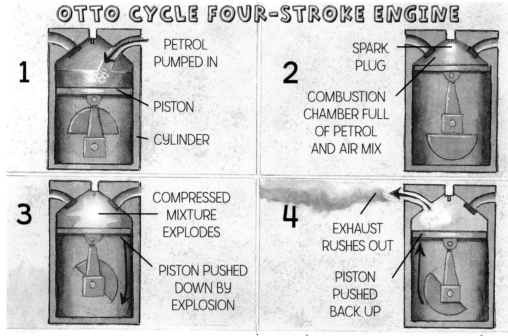

1 PETROL PUMPED IN — PISTON — CYLINDER

2 SPARK PLUG — COMBUSTION CHAMBER FULL OF PETROL AND AIR MIX

3 COMPRESSED MIXTURE EXPLODES — PISTON PUSHED DOWN BY EXPLOSION

4 EXHAUST RUSHES OUT — PISTON PUSHED BACK UP

In a steam engine (an external combustion engine) steam is pumped into the cylinder, which pushes the piston. In an internal combustion engine, something explosive is pumped into the cylinder and set on fire. The resulting explosion pushes the piston. In Germany Nikolaus Otto invented the four-stroke engine.

In about 1680, Christian Hugyens put gunpowder in a cylinder and set fire to it. We don't really know what happened but he didn't die for another 15 years – so the explosion can't have been too bad!

Several people worked out how to make different parts of the internal combustion engine work best. Some were known to each other, some unknown. After working with Otto, Gottlieb Daimler and Wilhelm Maybach bought a cottage in Stuttgart and built a workshop in the garden. Working long hours, the neighbours became convinced they must be forging money. But when the police raided the house, they found only engines.

The neighbours must have been even more amazed by the first motor bike!

ROAD RAGE

The motor car as we know it today went through many stages of development. The first cars were steam powered.

After building his road-running Puffing Devil and London Steam Carriage, Richard Trevithick decided they'd work best on railway lines.

Sir Goldsworthy Gurney built his Steam Carriage in 1825 putting an engine where the horse had been. It went at 20 miles per hour on public roads. He drove from London to Bath but crashed into the mail coach near Reading and was attacked by an angry mob. He needed an armed guard by the time he got to Bath.

In 1870, Siegfried Marcus of Germany put an internal combustion engine on a handcart but it didn't work very well.

It's for my wife's birthday.

Little do they know we are inventing the motor car!

In 1886, Daimler and Maybach bought a stagecoach. To avoid more trouble with the neighbours they told them it was Mrs Daimler's birthday present. They put an engine in it and created a motor car. At almost exactly the same time another German, Karl Benz, also built a car.

The Irish scientist, Mary Ward, became the first person to be killed in a car accident when she was thrown from a steam car in 1869.

Bridget Driscoll was the first person to be killed by a petrol driven car in 1896. It was only going at four miles per hour. The coroner told the driver that he hoped such a thing would never happen again. Today more people in the world die in car accidents than from any other cause.

FEATHERS, BIRDS AND BATS

It is thought that the Wright brothers made the first powered flight in 1903 – though quite a few people claimed to have got off the ground long before.

SIR GEORGE CAYLEY
(1773-1857)

Sir George Cayley's designs had all the features of a modern aeroplane. It certainly would have flown if he'd known of the internal combustion engine.

As a boy Sir George made a helicopter from a cork and some feathers.

In 1849, the ten-year-old son of one of Sir George's servants became the first person to fly in a glider he designed. Four years later he built a triplane. His coachman flew 275 metres before crashing, making him the first adult to fly a plane ... and crash. We know it could fly because in 1974 an exact replica flew OK.

CAPT JEAN-MARIE LE BRIS (1817-1872)

I think I've discovered the secret of flight.

Captain Le Bris, curious to know how albatrosses flew so effortlessly beside his speeding ship, once shot one. When he took its wing and held it in the wind, he noticed it began to rise into the air.

Back in France he wasted no time in building a large albatross from wood, sailcloth and rigging. He had this lifted onto a horse and cart and set off into the wind. Watching crowds gasped as he tilted the wings and the albatross soared heavenwards. But the driver of the cart got entangled in a dangling rope. After Jean-Marie had returned the terrified driver to earth, without his balancing weight, the albatross crashed into the ground and broke its wing.

For his next attempt, the captain launched the albatross over a deep quarry. It flew beautifully until it hit an air pocket and plunged to the bottom, shattering into a thousand pieces and breaking the Captain's leg.

Twelve years later he tried again. The bird flew to a height of 50 metres but then suddenly plummeted and once more shattered into pieces. After that he gave up … Terrible luck!

CLEMENT ADAIR
(1841-1926)

Clement felt that by copying nature he could build a machine in which humans might fly. He travelled far in this quest even observing vultures in the remote mountains of Algeria.

But on his return to France he modelled his first flying machine on a bat. The Eole even had folding wings. It was powered by a steam engine. In 1890 two of his friends claimed he made the first ever powered flight in an aeroplane … and crashed.

His next machine, Avion, had two engines. In 1897 he showed it to some French Army Generals. Avion got airborne but was blown sideways … and crashed. The Generals had seen a few hops – but were they big enough to count as flight?

ROARING INTO THE JET AGE

Taming the roar power of the gas turbine so it could be used in an aeroplane took a man with a lot of patience.

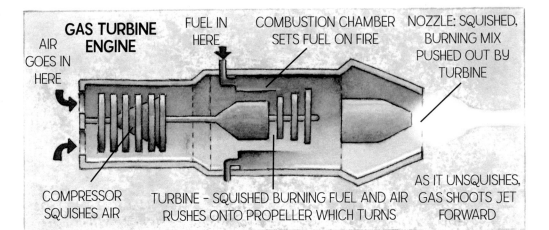

GAS TURBINE ENGINE

AIR GOES IN HERE

FUEL IN HERE

COMBUSTION CHAMBER SETS FUEL ON FIRE

NOZZLE: SQUISHED, BURNING MIX PUSHED OUT BY TURBINE

COMPRESSOR SQUISHES AIR

TURBINE – SQUISHED BURNING FUEL AND AIR RUSHES ONTO PROPELLER WHICH TURNS

AS IT UNSQUISHES, GAS SHOOTS JET FORWARD

The gas turbine was first thought up in England in 1791 by John Barber. His contraption didn't look much like an aeroplane engine!

FRANK WHITTLE
(1907-1996)
The inventor who never gave up.

You must work harder, Whittle.

Frank's teachers didn't know he spent every spare minute reading about aeroplanes or making models.

You're too short, Whittle!

All he wanted was to join the British Royal Air Force but he was only five feet tall. He trained like a maniac and grew another three inches. He applied three times before he was accepted.

He's too close to the ground.

At RAF college he became a daring pilot. He once got into trouble for hedgehopping.

It'll never work!

He also wrote an essay about aeroplanes with gas turbines. A man from the British government read it.

Frank was given a job testing biplanes to see if they would float when driven off an aircraft carrier. He didn't tell anybody that he couldn't swim.

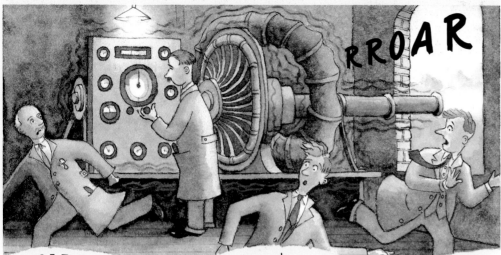

In 1935 Frank got some backing and found an old factory where he could build a jet engine. During its first test, it roared out of control. Everybody scattered, certain it was going to explode. Frank patiently worked on until he found ways to control it.

When the Second World War broke out, the government decided perhaps his engine could help win the war. They sent in such a crowd of experts that some ended up working on the stairs to Frank's office.

It's too quiet. I can't sleep!

The neighbours got so used to engines being tested day and night that they complained of being woken by the sudden silence when they stopped.

The jets gave off so much heat that a bush outside decided to flower in mid-winter.

Frank never gave up. In 1941 a small plane, fitted with one of his engines, took off.

HANS VON OHAIN
(1911-1998)

When you've fixed the oil leak, could you help me build a rocket?

Frank had no idea that, at the same time, Hans von Ohain, a German student, was building a very similar engine with the help of his car mechanic. An experimental plane, using his engine, flew three years before Frank's but the Second World War put a stop to his plans.

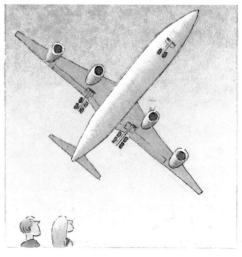

Nobody at the time realised that Frank's design would launch the jet age.

THE COMET'S DIFFICULT BIRTH

None of today's thousands of jet airliners could fly safely if it were not for the lessons learnt from the Comet.

"People won't want to fly around in jet planes!"

"Ridiculous idea!"

In the 1940s, the idea that anybody except the air force and a few very rich people might be able to fly around in jet planes seemed ridiculous.

The British Government decided a small jet plane to carry mail quickly across the Atlantic was needed. Lots of designs were considered.

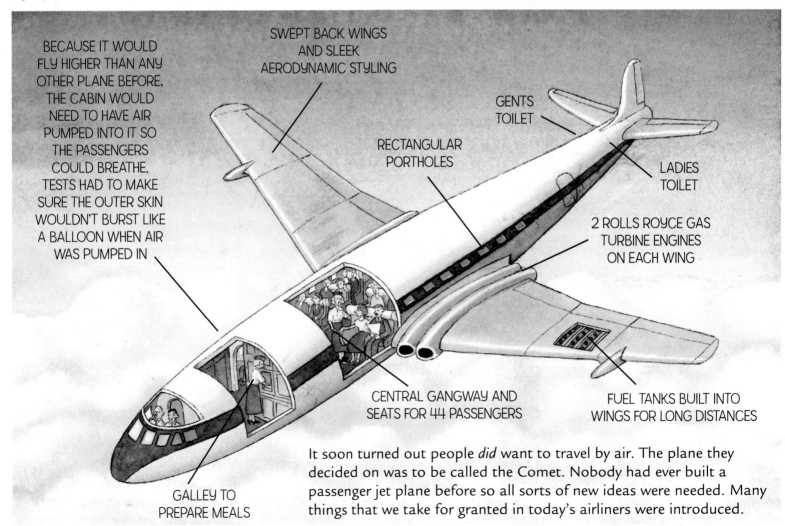

BECAUSE IT WOULD FLY HIGHER THAN ANY OTHER PLANE BEFORE, THE CABIN WOULD NEED TO HAVE AIR PUMPED INTO IT SO THE PASSENGERS COULD BREATHE. TESTS HAD TO MAKE SURE THE OUTER SKIN WOULDN'T BURST LIKE A BALLOON WHEN AIR WAS PUMPED IN

SWEPT BACK WINGS AND SLEEK AERODYNAMIC STYLING

RECTANGULAR PORTHOLES

GENTS TOILET

LADIES TOILET

2 ROLLS ROYCE GAS TURBINE ENGINES ON EACH WING

CENTRAL GANGWAY AND SEATS FOR 44 PASSENGERS

FUEL TANKS BUILT INTO WINGS FOR LONG DISTANCES

GALLEY TO PREPARE MEALS

It soon turned out people *did* want to travel by air. The plane they decided on was to be called the Comet. Nobody had ever built a passenger jet plane before so all sorts of new ideas were needed. Many things that we take for granted in today's airliners were introduced.

In May 1952 the very first Comet took off from Heathrow Airport, London. The age of the passenger jet had begun.

But in October a Comet crashed during take-off. The following year, three more Comets crashed. A lot of tests were done to find out what had gone wrong and some changes were made.

Then at the beginning of 1954 another two Comets crashed, both times killing everybody on board.

Any wreckage that could be recovered was inspected. On one crashed Comet, paint flecks from the fuselage were found on the tailplane. This showed that the fuselage had burst, spraying the paint backwards.

A huge water tank was built. A Comet was placed in it and pressurized. After several hours bubbles were seen at the corners of the square windows which showed the skin was cracking.

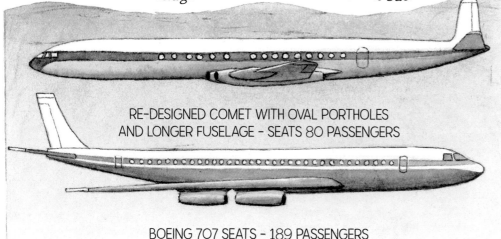

RE-DESIGNED COMET WITH OVAL PORTHOLES AND LONGER FUSELAGE - SEATS 80 PASSENGERS

BOEING 707 SEATS - 189 PASSENGERS

After other tests, the Comet was redesigned. Although it had got a bad reputation, many lessons were learnt from the Comet which make jet flight safer today. In 1958, a Comet made the first transatlantic flight – just one month before the American Boeing 707. The 707 was less expensive to run than the Comet, and over a thousand were made before production ended in 1978.

Although the Comet lost out, the RAF still flies Nimrods, which are basically the same as the Comet – the first ever jetliner.

AMAZING ROCKETS

A rocket is a tube with a small hole in the bottom. Burning gas inside is forced out, which pushes the rocket away.

A thousand years ago the Chinese discovered gunpowder and began making fireworks. The rocket probably got invented by accident.

ROAR!

That's amazing!

WAN HU – THE FIRST ASTRONAUT?

Legend tells us that a Chinese official, named Wan Hu, built himself a flying chair with kites for wings and 47 rockets attached. Forty-seven assistants lit the 47 fuses at exactly the same moment then raced for cover. A blinding flash ... a deafening roar ... when the smoke cleared there was no sign of Wan Hu or the chair. We'll never know if he was the first man in space – or blown to smithereens.

KONSTANTIN TSIOLKOVSKY
(1857-1935)

Konstantin Tsiolkovsky was a Russian maths teacher who dreamt about space travel in his spare time. He realised the way to put a satellite in orbit would be on top of a liquid fuel rocket in stages. As each stage burnt up it would fall away, reducing the weight for the next stage to push.

A rocket fired sideways from a mountain will go as far as the exploding fuel can push before falling to earth because of gravity.

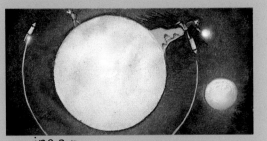

Imagine a mountain so high that it's almost beyond Earth's gravity. The rocket would travel round the earth in orbit and only fall back slowly.

Konstantin had other dreams:
- The nations of earth uniting to put a space station in orbit.
- A space elevator in an extremely tall version of the Eiffel Tower.
- A three-stage rocket.

MAN WILL CONQUER SPACE!

MAN WILL CONQUER SPACE   BY WERNHER VON BRAUN

In 1952 a magazine article told how man would soon travel into space with pictures of space stations, moon-landing craft and moon bases. Although written by Wernher Von Braun, a rocket designer working for the American army, many of the ideas came from books by Konstantin Tsiolkovsky.

THE SPACE RACE

After the Second World War ended the Americans and Russians began building rockets to launch weapons against each other – in case of a new war. There was one man working for each side who, more than anything, wanted those rockets to launch men into space.

WERNHER VON BRAUN (1912-1977)

Yikes!

WHOOSH

Wernher built his first rocket ship as a child in Germany. He and his brother tied six large fireworks to their go-cart and crashed into a grocer's shop.

Perhaps that'll stop him playing with fireworks!

It's a bit small. I can't see much.

Next, Wernher's parents bought him a telescope.

I wouldn't need a telescope to see the moon if I could go there.

Then Wernher read Konstantin Tsiolkovsky's books about space travel.

If only it was going into space.

By the age of 20 he'd become chief rocket designer for the German army. During the Second World War he worked on rockets to carry bombs.

The Russians will win control of space unless you let me launch a satellite.

By 1955 he was designing a three-stage rocket, called Jupiter, which he knew would be powerful enough to carry a satellite into space.

If only the Americans would let me build a moon rocket.

After the war, he moved to the USA to work on rockets to carry bombs for the American army.

It's so realistic!

I didn't know men had been to Mars!

He also advised Walt Disney on some films about space travel, which made the idea very popular in America.

SERGEI KOROLEV
(1907-1966)

As a teenager in the Soviet Union, Sergei lived near a seaplane base. Often he would swim across the bay for a closer look.

One day one of the pilots took him for a ride. Sergei was hooked.

While still at school Sergei built a glider. At college he read Konstantin's books and went on to find work designing rockets to carry bombs.

But Soviet Russia was a dangerous place. He was sent to a prison camp for designing rockets which used liquid instead of solid fuel! He nearly died.

After his release five years later he was made Chief Rocket Designer. By 1955 he had designed the R7, a rocket surrounded by boosters, which he knew could launch a satellite. He kept trying to persuade the Soviet government to let him.

SPUTNIK

Finally, in 1957 Sergei was allowed to launch an R7 with a football-sized sputnik on top. 'Sputnik' means satellite in Russian. Sergei's team waited nervously for the beeping radio signal, which would mean the first man-made object ever had reached orbit in outer space.

All over the world people watched for Sputnik and listened for the beep. Wernher was furious. He'd already built his three-stage Jupiter rocket, which he knew could launch a satellite.

Two months later an American rocket, built by the Navy, failed to launch. When the smoke cleared the satellite fell off the top and rolled away.

Oh! What a Flopnik!

The US government turned to Wernher. Next year his Jupiter rocket launched an American satellite into space.

ANIMALS IN SPACE

Both the Russians and Americans wanted to know if living creatures could survive in space so they sent up animals to find out.

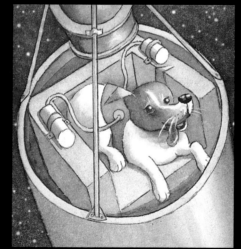

A Russian dog named Laika was the first animal in space. TV pictures showed her inside Sputnik II looking perfectly happy until the cooling system went wrong. Poor Laika got too hot and died. Two more dogs died before Strelka and Belka were successfully parachuted back to earth.

The USA wanted to know if a man would be able to work his controls OK in space. They trained a chimp, named Ham, to work some levers with a banana reward for a right lever and an electric shock in his foot for a wrong one. In space the machine kept giving Ham shocks even for the right lever. He got back OK but with a sore head and a very sore foot.

One shredded cabbage, one chopped onion ...

Ivan was a hollow dummy who the Russians filled with mice, guinea pigs, lizards and snakes and a tape recorder reciting a recipe for cabbage soup to test the radio.

IVAN IVANOVICH

... two diced carrots, three large potatoes ...

For company he had a dog named Blackie. They all returned from space in good health except Blackie, who ate all the foam lining inside the capsule and was sick. Ivan parachuted back to earth near a remote village where he lay twitching as the mice ran around inside him.

ASTRONAUTS AND COSMONAUTS

The Russian men chosen to go into space were called Cosmonauts (universe sailors) and the Americans astronauts (star sailors). In both countries doctors decided it was necessary to perform all sorts of strange tests on them.

They were shut in dark rooms for days on end.

Cold water was poured into their ears to see if their eyes fluttered!

The Earth looks very beautiful.

Sergei won this race. In 1961 Yuri Gagarin was the first man in space. Shortly after, American president John F Kennedy announced that America would land a man on the moon and bring him back safely. Between 1969 and 1972 six Apollo spacecraft landed on the moon.

What's the capital of the USA?

... Er

Moscow

They were asked questions while a voice whispered the wrong answer.

They were spun till their eyes nearly popped out.

41

Neil Armstrong on Apollo 11 was the first man to set foot on the Moon in July 1969.

COMMAND MODULE [CM] 3 CREW MEMBERS

COMMAND MODULE PARACHUTES FOR LANDING BACK ON EARTH

SERVICE MODULE [SM] OXYGEN & POWER SUPPLY. DISCARDED BEFORE RE-ENTRY

LUNAR MODULE [LM] 2 CREW MEMBERS

JUPITER ROCKET

EARTH

To carry the Apollo craft into space, Wernher set to work to build the enormous Saturn V rocket. It's still the biggest engine ever. The hangar it was built in was so tall, clouds were said to form on the ceiling.

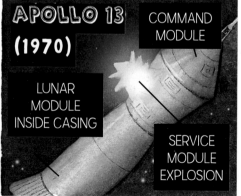

APOLLO 13 (1970)

COMMAND MODULE

LUNAR MODULE INSIDE CASING

SERVICE MODULE EXPLOSION

Halfway to the moon an oxygen tank in the Service Module exploded. The crew crawled into the Lunar Module to conserve air and power but it only had enough clean air to keep two people alive for two days.

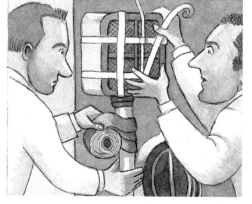

Instead of landing, Apollo 13 swung round the moon and back towards Earth. The crew taped bits and pieces together to make the air cleaners in the Command Module work in the Lunar Module.

They moved back into the Command Module for re-entry as only it had a heat shield. When the Service Module was ejected they saw how badly damaged it was. They splashed down safely in the Pacific.

INTERNATIONAL SPACE STATION

In 1993 the Russians and Americans decided to work together to build a space station just as Konstantin Tsilkovsky had dreamt. Although still being built, it's the largest man-made object in the sky. It can be seen with the naked eye when the sun is at the right angle. The first crew went up in 2000. Astronauts from 15 countries have visited. Studies are made to see how living in space for a long time affects the human body so that one day man can travel further and faster to Mars and beyond.

GOLF IN SPACE

In 1971 Alan Shepherd of Apollo 14 hit two golfballs on the moon. Without the Earth's gravity they went over two miles. In 2006, Russian Mikhail Tyurin hit a golf ball while being held by the legs from the ISS. The ball is still in orbit.

THE SPACE SHUTTLE

These reusable spaceships were first launched in 1981 and have flown over 100 successful missions especially to service the ISS.

THE SPACE SHUTTLE DISASTERS

Tragically, the second Shuttle Challenger exploded just after take off and the first, Columbia, broke up on re-entry in 2003 after completing 28 missions. Both their crews were killed. Space travel is still very dangerous. The shuttle is being replaced by Orion which is much more like the Apollo craft in design.

THE SHAPE OF THINGS TO COME

Travel may be very different in the future if these ideas can all be made to work as well as is hoped!

If you turn a magnet round it will push away a piece of metal, which was attracted to it.

MAGNET TRAINS

How can we stop it flying off the rails?

In 1904 an American student, Robert Goddard, had the idea that if you magnetized a railway track you could force a train to levitate (which means 'to float up') above the track. He called it Maglev. The problem would be keeping it there!

It was over 60 years before the first passenger-carrying Maglev train ran in Shanghai, China, at speeds of over 500 kilometres per hour.

There are now plans for lines in several other countries. Perhaps one day all trains will be Maglev.

My plane doesn't seem to want to land!

A plane flying just above the ground can stay airborne with very little engine power. It's called Wing in Ground Effect (WIG).

SEA MONSTERS!

In 1967 American spy satellite photos showed several enormous planes skimming across the Caspian Sea in Russia. They nicknamed these ekranoplans 'Caspian Sea Monsters'. Although they didn't work very well, the Russians built them bigger and bigger ... until in 1980 the biggest of all crashed, and they gave up.

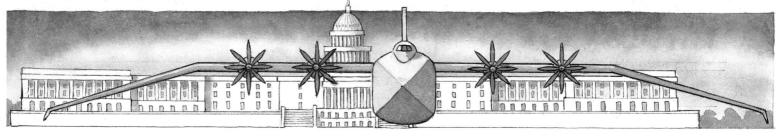

Today Boeing are experimenting with a plane named Pelican after the birds which use the wing in ground effect to skim over water. It's also known as ULTRA (Ultra Large Transport Aircraft).

It will be as wide as the Capitol building in Washington, carry ten times as much as any current aircraft, be ten times faster than a ship and have 76 wheels.

FLYING FASTER

Ever since Comet, jet airliners have looked like a tube with wings and a tailplane. Many designers believe that a simple flying wing would be more efficient. But planes of this shape have proved hard to control. Boeing are developing a blended wing body, which is halfway between a flying wing and an existing airliner. Passengers will be seated inside the wing. Perhaps all airliners of the future will be this shape.

PLUNGING DEEPER

There is still a huge area of the Earth left to explore – the ocean bed. Since the 1960s an American submersible called Alvin has been diving into the deep. The Human Occupied Vehicle, Alvin's replacement, can dive much deeper and will be able to explore nearly all the floors of all the oceans. It has a pilot and two observers. Who knows what they'll find down there?

SAILING FURTHER

If light from the sun hits a mirror floating in space, it acts like wind on a sail and pushes the mirror forward. This energy is very slight but it's free. A solar sail consists of huge mirrors made from very light sheeting, which will unfurl in space. At first the sail would move very slowly but, with constant light from the sun, it would gradually travel faster and faster until it could travel further into outer space than any vehicles before. Some unmanned spacecraft have already used solar sails to make small manoeuvres in space.

RISING HIGHER

Just as Konstantin Tsiolkovsky's dream of an international space station became reality so one day may his space elevator. Researchers are already developing a very fine, light cable which could be carried up by a rocket and tethered to a space station in orbit. Once the first cable was in place, more and more fine cables could be dragged up the first and woven together into one very big cable. Vehicles could run up and down this like the cars in a lift.

Going up!

FASTER, FURTHER INTO THE FUTURE!

WORMHOLES

Scientists have worked out there must be shortcuts in space, though nobody has ever seen one. They named them wormholes because space is curved like the skin of an apple. A worm burrowing through an apple would reach the other side much faster than one that wriggled round the outside. Even at the speed of light it would take four years to reach the star nearest to our sun. If we want to travel further in a lifetime, wormholes might be the only way ... could it be possible one day?

TIME TRAVEL

How could we travel through time? There are several ideas ... they are *not* easy to understand!

If you could put people to sleep and stop them ageing, they might wake up far in the future but no older.

Travelling in a rocket at the speed of light, time would pass more slowly than in the place you left. When you got back, you'd be younger than your stay-at-home friends – as though you'd travelled into the future.

Some say time travel is impossible, or people from the future would already have visited *us*. As far as we know, nobody has yet!

TELEPORTATION

Photos are sent over the internet as digital code. An exact copy is put back together on the other person's computer screen. Could you send a whole human being as digital code so they could exist in two places at once? Would the copy really be exactly the same person?

VIRTUAL TRAVEL

We can already see and hear the virtual worlds of computer games. Suppose we could also touch, smell and feel our bodies moving in them. Perhaps then we'd never feel the need to leave our armchairs to travel faster, further, higher or deeper again!

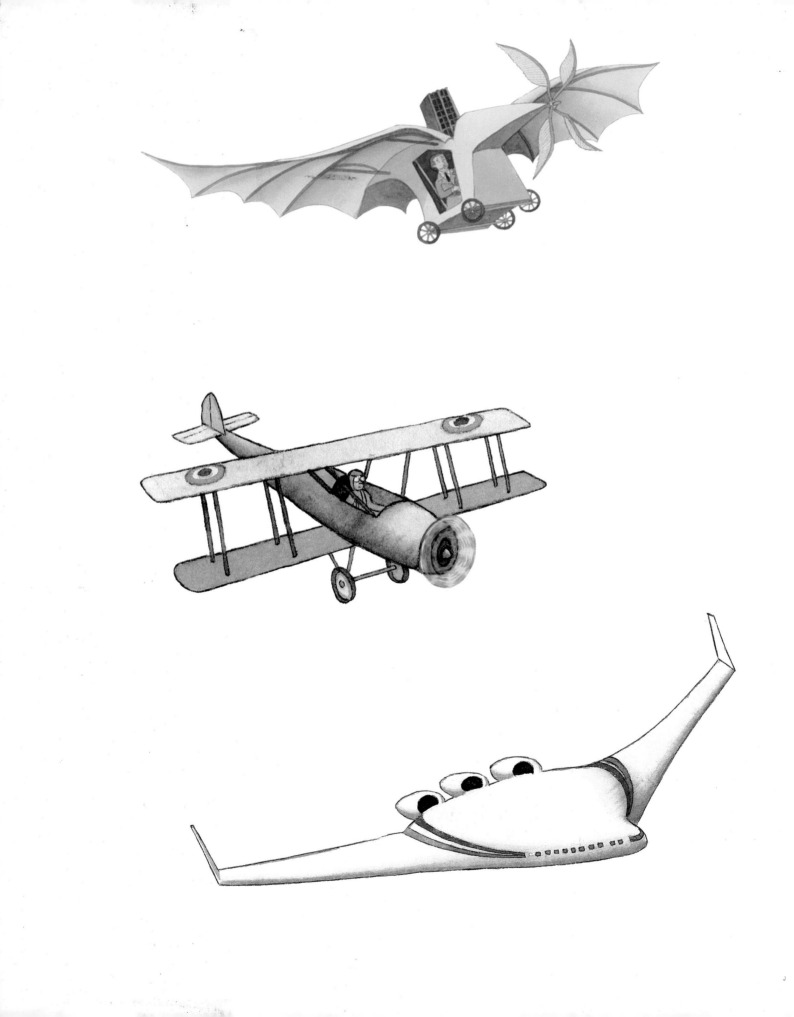